In 90 Days

In 90 Days

What Will You Do?

In 90 Days

In 90 Days

What Will You Do?

By

Onedia N. Gage, Ph. D., CLC

In 90 Days

Scriptures

Then the Lord replied: "Write the vision and make it plain."

Habakkuk 2:2

"For I know the plans that I have for you," declares the Lord, "Plans to prosper you and not to harm you, plans to give you hope and a future."

Jeremiah 29:11

No, in all things we are more than conquerors through Him who loved us.

Romans 8:37

In 90 Days

DEDICATION

To the dreamers

To the achievers

To those who just need a nudge

To those who need a push

To those who lead by example

To those who encourage achievement

To Jordan and Nehemiah

I hope that I have given you everything

You need to have the courage to dream

And the boldness to achieve those dreams

LIBRARY OF CONGRESS

In 90 Days:

What Will You Do?

All Rights Reserved © 2022

Onedia N. Gage, Ph. D., CLC

No part of this book may be reproduced or transmitted in
Any form or by any means, graphic, electronic, or mechanical,
Including photocopying, recording, taping, or by any
Information storage or retrieval system, without the
Permission in writing from the publisher.

Purple Ink, Inc. Press

For Information address:
Purple Ink, Inc.
10223 Broadway St., Ste. P292
Pearland, TX 77584
www.purpleink.net ♦ onediagage@purpleink.net

Onedia Gage Speaks

www.onediagagespeaks.com ♦ onediagage@onediagagespeaks.com

ISBN:

978-1-939119-64-3

Printed in the United States

Other Books by Onedia N. Gage, Ph. D.

Are You Ready for 9th Grade . . . Again? A Family's Guide to Success
As We Grow Together Daily Devotional for Expectant Couples
As We Grow Together Prayer Journal for Expectant Couples
As We Grow Together Bible Study: Her Workbook
As We Grow Together Bible Study: His Workbook
The Best 40 Days of My Life: A Journey of Spiritual Renewal
The Blue Print: Poetry for the Soul
From Fat to Fit in 90 Days: A Fitness Journal
From Two to One: The Notebook for the Christian Couple
Hannah's Voice: Powerful Lessons in Prayer
The Heart of a Woman: The Depth of Her Spirit (Poetry)
Her Story The Legacy of Her Fight: The Bible Study
Her Story The Legacy of Her Fight: The Devotional
Her Story The Legacy of Her Fight: The Legacy Journal
Her Story The Legacy of Her Fight: Prayers and Journal
I Am.: 90 Days of Powerful Words: Affirmation and Advice for Girls
ILY! A Mother Daughter Relationship Workbook
In Her Own Words: Notebook for the Christian Woman
In Purple Ink: Poetry for the Spirit
In Your Hands: A Dad's Impact on Your Daughter's Self-Esteem
Intensive Couples Retreat: Her Workbook
Intensive Couples Retreat: His Workbook
Living A Whole Life: Sermons Which Prompt, Provoke and Provide Life
Love Letters to God from a Teenage Girl
The Measure of a Woman: The Details of Her Soul
The Notebook: For Me, About Me, By Me
The Notebook for the Christian Teen
On This Journey Daily Devotional for Young People
On This Journey Prayer Journal for Young People
On This Journey Prayer Journal for Young People, Vol. 2
One Day More Than We Deserve Prayer Journal for the Growing Christian
Promises, Promises: A Novel
Queen in the Making: 30 Week Bible Study for Teen Girls
Queen in the Making: 30 Week Bible Study for Teen Girls Leader's Guide
There's a Queen Within: Her Journey to Self—Worth
She Spoke Volumes . . . And Then Some
Six Months of Solitude: The Sanctity of Singleness Notebook
Six Months of Solitude: The Sanctity of Singleness Prayers and Journal
Tools for These Times: Timely Sermons for Uncertain Times

With An Anointed Voice: The Power of Prayer
A Woman Like Me: A Bible Study
A Woman Like Me: A Daily Devotional
A Woman Like Me: A Sermonic Study
Yielded and Submitted: A Woman's Journey for a Life Dedicated to God
Yielded and Submitted: A Woman's Journey for a Life Dedicated to God An Intimate Study
Yielded and Submitted: A Woman's Journey for a Life Dedicated to God Prayers and Journal

The Nehemiah Character Series

Nehemiah and His Basketball
Nehemiah and His Big Sister
Nehemiah and His Bike
Nehemiah and His Flag Football Team
Nehemiah and His Football
Nehemiah and His Golf Clubs
Nehemiah and Math
Nehemiah and the Bully
Nehemiah and the Busy Day
Nehemiah and the Class Field Trip
Nehemiah and the Substitute for the Substitute
Nehemiah Can Swim
Nehemiah Found the Mud
Nehemiah Reads to Mommy
Nehemiah Writes Just Like Mommy
Nehemiah, the Hot Dog, and the Broccoli
Nehemiah's Family Vacation
Nehemiah's Favorite Teacher Returns to School
Nehemiah's First Day of School
Nehemiah's Sister Moved
Nehemiah's Visit to the Hospital

WHAT WILL YOU DO?

In 90 Days

TABLE OF CONTENTS

Author's Address	17
Why 90 Days?	19
No More Excuses	21
Dreams vs. Goals	25
The Goals Revised	31
The First Step	37
90 Days: Plan Your Work	43
Launch the 90 Days	49
90 Day Plan vs. 90 Day Actual	53
The Plan	59
The Execution	67
The Results	73
The Celebration	79
Repeat: The 90 Days Restarted	83
90 Days in Review: "How do you do it?"	87
Appendix	93

IN 90 DAYS

ACKNOWLEDGEMENTS 121

ABOUT THE ACHIEVER 123

Dear Future 90 Day-er,

As the author of over 100 published books, including eBooks, I am always asked, "How do you do it?" That is an easy answer, but when I share the answer, the other person finds it really hard to understand and to hear and to do. I am not sure why, but they do.

I do understand that some things are harder to accomplish than others, however, I cannot understand wanting something and never starting the project.

Being focused is the first priority of accomplishment. Sacrifice is the next action. Taking action is the next part. Completion. Follow up. These are the elements that make success possible.

I know that you will start and want to quit, and maybe even actually, quit. But after a short time, you need to resume your quest. You want to achieve greatness. Your pursuit of greatness requires work, diligence, tiring, sometimes fruitless, work. When you respond to the calling of the creations and entrepreneurship, you will be disappointed and happy, worried and fulfilled, exhausted and exhilarated, all while spending all of your time and money on this pursuit.

Just know that it is worth it.

90 days seems so short depending on your perspective. So long on another perspective. It is a period of accomplishment. It is protecting your time and disciplining your attention span.

What will you accomplish in 90 Days? And the 90 days after that?

I dare you to try what I prescribe and what you are most afraid of: success.

See you at the top,

Onedia N. Gage, Ph. D., CLC

Parent. Speaker. Author. Publisher. Educator. Motivator. Coach.

In 90 Days

Why 90 Days?

Introduction

Consider your dreams and goals. Are you at a satisfaction level? If not, why not? What does it require to reach those dreams and goals? Why aren't you achieving your goals and dreams? Do you know? What do you want to change about achieving these goals?

What are you doing instead of achieving your goals? The first action item in order to achieve your goals is to eliminate obstacles. The first elimination is the television and societal media in excess. I only watched two hours of television each week for over a decade. One of the benefits of that discipline was 25 published books reaching over 100 books, and achieving the goals that I set.

How do I do it? Discipline. Plan. Work. Don't quit. Put my head down. Don't get distracted. Hard work. Work hard.

The first decision is to stop procrastinating. Making a list helps. Having a plan helps as well.

I want this book to become a springboard to achievement. Do everything it says. Follow up on your efforts. Watch you reach your goals and see the success that you dreamed of.

We are mostly driven by success and achievement. Once we start to achieve, we want to repeat that over and over again.

This will be rigorous.

This will be ridiculous.

This will be exciting.

This will be hard.

In 90 Days

This will be exhausting.

This will be rough.

This will be mentally taxing.

This will be overwhelming.

This will be amazing.

This will be fulfilling.

This will be awesome.

This will be exhilarating.

This will be exciting.

This will be satisfying.

I seek to give you the encouragement to proceed to pursue your life at the highest possible level, achieving the best possible results.

I don't have a person like me, so I want to give you the encouragement that I need in order to move forward with life.

I look forward to your outlandish pursuit so that you can achieve the impossible.

Follow all of the advice and instructions. This will be beneficial for the most efficient manner in which to achieve your goals.

Let's make these next 90 days the best 90 days ever.

No More Excuses

"I don't have time."

"I don't have the money."

"I don't have the right state of mind at this time."

"I don't know how."

"I don't know where to start."

"I have kids."

"I don't have kids."

"I am married."

"I am not married."

"I don't have good credit."

"I don't have any credit."

The excuses which have been standing in your way the entire time that you have desired this goal and dream have been stalled for any of those excuses and one hundred more possible excuses not mentioned here. Excuses are dream-diffusers and goal-killers. This is the first thing that stops you from reaching your goals and reaching your dreams.

There will be times when you will not be able to separate the excuses from the ability to start the process to achievement.

The first step to eliminating the excuses is to be able to recognize them as excuses. If you didn't need any additional money, and you would still want to pursue this goal and dream, then the money is the excuse. You may be thinking that money is a real issue. It may be temporary, however, let's address the money excuse.

Have you tried to save money? Have you tried to earn any extra money by implementing your goal/dream now on a small scale in order to raise the money and practice your craft?

Have you given this goal/dream your whole, persistent effort? Have you given this your 100% effort? If the answer is no, then you need to either eliminate the excuses or stop dreaming and goal making.

So for every excuse, then is a solution.

Find it.

Seek it.

Figure it out.

When you can answer the following questions, then you can reach your dreams/goals.

How badly do you really want this goal/dream? What will you do in order to achieve it? Who will help you to reach your goals/dreams? When will you stop making excuses and start doing the work which is required to achieve these goals and dreams?

When will you start?

REFLECTION

1. What are your excuses?
2. What is required to permanently eliminate each one?
3. How long do you need to eliminate those excuses?

Excuse	How to Eliminate	When can it be eliminated

"When I start every class, I share that I lead a no excuse offense. I am definitely not listening to your excuses. Further, I am not going to help enable you with those excuses."

Onedia N. Gage, Chief Achiever

Dreams vs. Goals

A dream is something that you want. Either a job, a car, or a material item, including a vacation. It is usually 'out of reach,' or it seems so based on some limiting factors.

Dreams do not seem to be achievable, maybe not even tangible. You may even compare yourself to others because they are achieving their dreams.

We dream from childhood. As early as you can remember, someone asked you what you wanted to be when you grow up, and other similar questions which they reminded you of periodically throughout your life. Whether the answers were reasonable or not, you were reminded and then held accountable for those answers.

When was the last time you reviewed your dreams? Have you eliminated anything on that list? Based on achieved or no longer interested in the dream?

Based on the dream list, what will you pursue on that list? List them in order of what will you pursue first.

Once you have made that list, then we are going to add a column for the date to be accomplished—this transitions the dream to a goal.

Goals are dreams with a date. The move from dream to the goal makes the work start.

Goals definitely require work. These goals will require a plan to achieve. Achieving your goals requires work—daily.

What will these goals lead to? A career? A new career? An entrepreneurial endeavor? A new home? A new car?

How do you reach those goals(s)? What knowledge do you need? Who can help you with it? How long will this work take to achieve this goal?

In 90 Days

What happens if you do not achieve the goal on the due date?

With the proper tools and knowledge and discipline, goals will be achieved, and in a timely manner. Achieving your goals means that you are an achiever. Further, it means that you are disciplined and did not quit.

The achievement has the ability to be repetitive. This goal achieved will bring you the success that you desire and deserve.

Make your list.

Assign them dates.

Do your research.

Plan your plan and your work.

Work your plan.

Don't quit.

Watch your work become results.

REFLECTION

Goal	Date	What's Needed	Who

In 90 Days

How do you feel about writing those goals down? What did this reveal to you?

_____

_____

_____

_____

How will this help you to be successful?

_____

_____

"I set goals all of the time. I achieve some of them on time; others I don't and on which am still working. But what is universal for all achievers is that we DON'T QUIT."

Onedia N. Gage

In 90 Days

THE GOALS REVISED

We learned and reviewed goals and goal setting. Now, we will revise, expand, and if you will, embrace those goals.

As an achiever, you will think outside of the previous norms, also known as the box. You will have to abandon the standard way of thinking.

The behavior becomes a dogmatic pursuit of the goal, rather than the slow, low maintenance progress that you have been making so far. To date, you have thought about your goals and your desires. To date, you have not really pursued the goal. Now, this is not how you pursue other interests. You are all in with other things that are not the goal. Consider this reason the goal has not been reached.

You have 90 days to reach this goal. You have 90 days to have this goal manifest itself into the best thing that has ever happened to you. Can you do it? Put aside your fears, doubts, and most of all your excuses for 90 days so that you can achieve the one thing that has been sitting in the pit of your stomach or at the back of your throat since you could remember. 90 days to the victory of the goal is within reach if you focus on the goal—solely and fiercely.

Your job for 90 days is to work on that ultimate goal and the winner mindset that you need to develop that business and stay in business.

The winner mindset requires development and training.

So, what is required to change the course of your life so that you can achieve your goal?

- Stop watching television
- Start researching the fees associated with starting a business
- Stop hanging out for more than three hours more than once each week
- Start saving the money to start the business
- Stop procrastinating

- Reroute your time into studying your competition and their successes and failure
- Start to behave like an actual business person
- Learn what a business owner does:
  - How long will you work?
  - How many vacations, recitals, ball games, and parent conferences may you miss?
  - How to be diplomatic, and calm in a crisis?
  - Who shows up when all of your employees are sick?
  - Study your craft
  - Study your industry
  - Know and understand your competition

Embrace the winner mindset. Stop putting yourself down. Stop doubting yourself. Stop questioning your abilities. Stop looking around. Stop doubting your intentions.

Employ the winner mindset. Start stating positive affirmations to yourself daily. Start making a list the night before of what you will accomplish the next day. Only a list of 5 to 6 things that you will do the next day. Start joining the business organizations. Start planning the family's schedule so that they are prepared for the changes that you all will face once you reach your goal. Start researching your virtual mentor—a business person who you admire and consider successful. Start considering a local mentor as well so that you can ask all of your questions—select someone who answers questions and provide advice. Start keeping a calendar so that you can be on time to all meetings and to ensure that you don't miss any meetings or events. Start focusing on your image so that you are taken seriously as you enter the next level.

Keep your family communication open and transparent. You will need them on your side for the future and all that the future holds.

Redesign your life so that achievement can happen.

- Omit the negative
- Stop playing games

- Stop procrastinating
- Start working on your goals like your life and livelihood depends on it
- Put your goals in front of you
    - Big paper on the walls so that you can see the goals on a large enough page so that you can see it daily should stimulate internal accountability which causes you pain when you do not do your job for the goals.

Reflection

1. Who is your biggest supporter?

_____

_____

2. Who is your biggest critic?

_____

_____

3. What is going to be the hardest thing to give up?

_____

_____

4. What part of your schedule is going to be the hardest to change?

_____

_____

5. Who can help you or mentor you through this transition?

_____

_____

6. Are you prepared to acquire professional assistance such as a coach in order to help facilitate your progress in your achievement?

_____

_____

"I've accomplished things that were not ever on my radar."

Onedia N. Gage

THE FIRST STEP

The first step to achieving the goal is continuing to the goal. You have to be all—in. You cannot hang on to the fence of whether you want to achieve that goal or not. You will NEVER achieve what you don't <u>completely</u> believe in. And you can't expect others to believe in what you are not committed to at 100%.

Don't get mad.

Don't get angry.

Don't get self-righteous.

Don't get confused.

All-in. If you waiver even a little bit, then you can forget the plans and efforts, energy and characteristic.

All-in. No quitting. No unraveling. No questions. No second thoughts.

All-in.

All-in.

First step: commitment.

First step: focus.

First step: priority.

First step: sacrifice.

First step: eat your goal.

First step: sleep your goal.

First step: breathe your goal.

If you are not talking about your goal daily. All day. Everyday. Then you are not all in. You cannot pursue your goal with the safety of a backup plan.

All in is not the existence or the pursuit of a backup plan.

The First Step: Fully Commit.

No excuses.

No backup plans.

No backing up.

No backing out.

Mash the gas.

Give it all you have got.

If you don't give it all that you have within and the energy it deserves and requires; then you will not gain the respect you believe that you deserve.

No one will take you seriously if you are not all in.

So, if you are not all in, then don't waste your time at all.

REFLECTION

1. There are eight First Steps listed. Order them in order for which is going to be hardest to do first.

_____

_____

_____

_____

_____

_____

_____

2. What is your plan for overcoming your biggest obstacle?

_____

_____

3. What will you do for encouragement on the hardest part of your journey?

_____

_____

4. What is preventing you from achieving the goals which you have set forth?

_____

_____

"You can always start with being honest with yourself today!"

Onedia N. Gage

In 90 Days

90 Days: Plan Your Work

Day 1: Write the vision of your goal.

Day 2: Establish a date done by. Preferably 90 days.

Day 3: _____

Day 4: _____

Day 5: _____

Day 6: _____

Day 7: _____

Day 8: _____

Day 9: _____

Day 10: _____

Day 11: _____

Day 12: _____

Day 13: _____

Day 14: _____

Day 15: _____

Day 16: _____

Day 17: _____

In 90 Days

Day 18: _____

Day 19: _____

Day 20: _____

Day 21: _____

Day 22: _____

Day 23: _____

Day 24: _____

Day 25: _____

Day 26: _____

Day 27: _____

Day 28: _____

Day 29: _____

Day 30: _____

Day 31: _____

Day 32: _____

Day 33: _____

Day 34: _____

Day 35: _____

Day 36: _____

WHAT WILL YOU DO?

Day 37: _____

Day 38: _____

Day 39: _____

Day 40: _____

Day 41: _____

Day 42: _____

Day 43: _____

Day 44: _____

Day 45: _____

Day 46: _____

Day 47: _____

Day 48: _____

Day 49: _____

Day 50: _____

Day 51: _____

Day 52: _____

Day 53: _____

Day 54: _____

Day 55: _____

In 90 Days

Day 56: _____

Day 57: _____

Day 58: _____

Day 59: _____

Day 60: _____

Day 61: _____

Day 62: _____

Day 63: _____

Day 64: _____

Day 65: _____

Day 66: _____

Day 67: _____

Day 68: _____

Day 69: _____

Day 70: _____

Day 71: _____

Day 72: _____

Day 73: _____

Day 74: _____

WHAT WILL YOU DO?

Day 75: _____

Day 76: _____

Day 77: _____

Day 78: _____

Day 79: _____

Day 80: _____

Day 81: _____

Day 82: _____

Day 83: _____

Day 84: _____

Day 85: _____

Day 86: _____

Day 87: _____

Day 88: _____

Day 89: _____

Day 90: _____

"I am only at risk to succeed."

Onedia N. Gage

Launch the 90 Days

What will you do with your 90 days?

Do you have what is required to finish your goal(s) in 90 days?

Your answer needs to be YES. A resounding, absolute loud, scream to the TOP of your lungs—YES!

Do it NOW! SCREAM YES!

1. Make a list of what you need to achieve your goal(s).

_____
_____
_____
_____

2. Make an announcement to your family, friends, co-workers, and all persons of significance that you have a goal.

_____
_____
_____
_____

IN 90 DAYS

3. Write your daily schedule so that you will be able to stick to it and achieve your goal(s).

_____

_____

_____

_____

_____

"The future I have ahead of me cannot afford for me to quit.

There ain't no quit in me!"

Onedia N. Gage

In 90 Days

90 Day Plan vs 90 Day Actual

What did you actually do in comparison to the plan?

Day 1: _____

Day 2: _____

Day 3: _____

Day 4: _____

Day 5: _____

Day 6: _____

Day 7: _____

Day 8: _____

Day 9: _____

Day 10: _____

Day 11: _____

Day 12: _____

Day 13: _____

Day 14: _____

Day 15: _____

In 90 Days

Day 16: _____

Day 17: _____

Day 18: _____

Day 19: _____

Day 20: _____

Day 21: _____

Day 22: _____

Day 23: _____

Day 24: _____

Day 25: _____

Day 26: _____

Day 27: _____

Day 28: _____

Day 29: _____

Day 30: _____

Day 31: _____

Day 32: _____

Day 33: _____

Day 34: _____

What Will You Do?

Day 35: _____

Day 36: _____

Day 37: _____

Day 38: _____

Day 39: _____

Day 40: _____

Day 41: _____

Day 42: _____

Day 43: _____

Day 44: _____

Day 45: _____

Day 46: _____

Day 47: _____

Day 48: _____

Day 49: _____

Day 50: _____

Day 51: _____

Day 52: _____

Day 53: _____

In 90 Days

Day 54: _____

Day 55: _____

Day 56: _____

Day 57: _____

Day 58: _____

Day 59: _____

Day 60: _____

Day 61: _____

Day 62: _____

Day 63: _____

Day 64: _____

Day 65: _____

Day 66: _____

Day 67: _____

Day 68: _____

Day 69: _____

Day 70: _____

Day 71: _____

Day 72: _____

WHAT WILL YOU DO?

Day 73: _____

Day 74: _____

Day 75: _____

Day 76: _____

Day 77: _____

Day 78: _____

Day 79: _____

Day 80: _____

Day 81: _____

Day 82: _____

Day 83: _____

Day 84: _____

Day 85: _____

Day 86: _____

Day 87: _____

Day 88: _____

Day 89: _____

Day 90: _____

"Do it Big.

Do it Now.

Do it Afraid."

Onedia N. Gage

THE PLAN

If you were going to publish a book, then there is a plan. There are steps that need to be taken.

Writing the book is the hardest part. After writing 70 books, I am probably considered an expert on writing books.

Writing a book requires discipline. Discipline is defined as scheduling time to write the book. Schedule two hours each day for 30 days, which equals 60 hours of writing. That time should offer you a healthy manuscript. This discipline means that you give up television and other recreational activities in order to do that work.

This is the same requirement that is required for other goals. Realize that watching television is actually watching the manifestation of the goal of someone else. Shonda Rhimes created several television shows, but she did not create them by watching the shows of others. She created at least five shows. She owns Thursday night television on ABC. She did not get that position by not working daily. Daily. In a committed position to achieve her goals.

I started publishing books in 2000, after BEGGING traditional publishers to do so. After many non—responses, many no answers, and many returned letters, I started my own publishing firm. That time from 2000 to 2022, I have published 70 books, not including ebooks or the books of other authors.

I am committed to writing and publishing books. This however is the extension of a goal. I only wanted to publish two books—two.

Two (2) doesn't turn into seventy (70) without some discipline in the format of no television, missed sleep, missed vacations, and limited fun unless my children's presence was required. I schedule fun and there is not much spontaneity available.

However, I achieved things that I never thought possible—some of which I never even wanted to do.

Then after I wrote them, I published them. They are distributed worldwide and there is a check deposited in my account monthly. All because I took a chance, employed some discipline, and worked really hard. I did not develop a business plan or anything else formal.

So, imagine that you really commit to your goal, start believing that it will become a reality, put some GRIT into your work so that you see some results, and then continue to work until your goal becomes your daily life and your daily work.

What does your plan look like?

What does your strategy look like?

What accountability mechanisms do you have planned?

When I started my novel, my second book, I was writing and a friend asked me what I was writing. In response, I lied to her. I told her that I was writing my grocery list. She called me out about my lie, so I confessed. When I told her that did not want anyone to know so if I quit, no one would know that I had ever started.

She responded with that is exactly why you share with others what you are doing so that you can be accountable and so that you don't quit.

As you can tell that I did not quit but it did fuel a segment of my life that I NEVER anticipated; things I never dreamed of.

So, what is your plan?

How will you proceed?

Who will you tell first?

What will you say?

When I plan my projects, I have pages where I plan my work. How will you plan your work? How will you keep track of your progress?

I use lists and checklists. I write everything down so when I accomplish that item, I mark through it and place a date next to it.

So, schedule about 90 minutes to write out a plan for your plan.

IN 90 DAYS

REFLECTION

1. What is the goal(s)?

_____

_____

2. What is the due date(s)?

_____

_____

3. What skills do you need to complete that goal?
    a. Do you possess those skills which are required?

_____

_____

4. Who do you know that can assist you with this goal?

_____

_____

5. What materials are needed for the goal?

_____

_____

6. What is the process to achieve the goal?

_____

_____

7. How will you market the goal?

_____

_____

8. How do you make the goal happen?

_____

_____

9. How will you duplicate this for other goals?

_____

_____

In 90 Days

By When	Goal	Materials Needed	Process Steps to Achieve

What Will You Do?

Who Can Help to Achieve	How to Market the Goal	How to Make the Goal Happen

"My success and my desires, my personality, and my activities cause others to be able to be themselves as well."

Onedia N. Gage

THE EXECUTION OF THE PLAN

Once the plan is underway, what are the changes which have happened to make this goal head toward success and achievement? Does the family evening time frame change?

When I returned to graduate school, I selected an online class format. I completed all of my homework after 9:30 PM each night after my children were put to bed. This continued for nearly two years. It also meant that I went to bed later than I may have wanted. My goal was important because there was a career advancement and financial gains available as a result of that completed education.

The important part of this discussion is that the time frame of the completion was finite so I know that it was a certain period of time with a definite ending date.

That is different from other goals which do not end, such as starting a business, getting married, and having children.

The execution of the plan will require certain sacrifices from you and all related parties. What are those changes and who will be responsible for those changes?

How long will the changes be able to be sustained? How long will the goal take to achieve?

This is the time to be a FINISHER! Finish what you start. Finish the goal you pursue. You have to start and you have to finish. This is not exactly a choice.

In order to be an achiever, you have to finish. You CANNOT quit. You cannot abandon the course. It will be difficult, maybe even hard, but it is rewarding to reach the goal. It is fulfilling to reach the goal. It is closure to reach the goal.

It is never guessing or questioning what would it be like to complete the process in order to reach the goal. It is overcoming issues or obstacles or barriers to reaching a goal. It is the bravest act that you will ever do. Achievement requires courage. This may require all that you have within. This will require more than you ever had done before in any other situation. It will take all that you have. Sometimes. Often. Forever.

Starting. Working diligently. Finishing. Repeat. Your self—esteem will increase when you start seeing progress and meeting milestones. This will help you with motivation. You will need that motivation for the roughest of days: the days that you want to quit.

The execution of the plan to accomplish the goal includes research about the goal and the results. The research includes where will this goal be used and useful.

Will this goal expand/extend your career?

Does it garner additional income?

Does it expand your networking capacity?

Does it extend your territory?

Does it transform your future?

Does it create a legacy for your family? Your children?

Does it establish a heritage for your family? Does it change the financial future of your family?

Does your credit score and worthiness support the business funding needs?

Does your goal require that eventually, you quit your job?

How will your healthcare survive this goal achievement?

Who will publicize this accomplishment when this is done?

What will this cost you: financially? Emotionally? Timing? Time away from your family, work, or other obligations and responsibilities?

The execution of the plan will change your life and your view of that life. My goal sheet has all kinds of items on it, such as a law degree and fifty more books. The decision that I have to make is whether or not I actually decide to go to law school. I will also determine which, if not all, of those titles I will actually write and publish.

When you consider the goal and the age of the goal, can you reasonably achieve them all? Some cannot be achieved at particular stages in life. Some will wait and others will not.

What is your bandwidth and capacity for the time you will spend on this goal(s)?

Your family and inner circle will be tolerable as long as your endeavors do not interfere or derail life as they currently enjoy it.

Reflection

Will this goal expand/extend your career? If so, how?
_____
_____

Does it garner additional income? If so, how much? When will that change be effective?
_____
_____

Does it expand your networking capacity? How so?
_____
_____

Does it extend your territory? If so, how?
_____
_____

Does it transform your future? How so?
_____
_____

Does it create a legacy for your family? Your children? How so?
_____
_____

Does it establish a heritage for your family? Does it change the financial future of your family? How?

_____

_____

Does your credit score and worthiness support the business funding needs?

_____

_____

Does your goal require that eventually, you quit your job? How will you feel about that?

_____

_____

How will your healthcare survive this goal achievement? Will you need an independent plan?

_____

_____

Who will publicize this accomplishment when this is done?

_____

_____

What will this cost you: financially? Emotionally? Timing? Time away from your family, work, or other obligations and responsibilities?

_____

_____

"Just because I make this look easy does not mean it is."
Onedis N. Gage

THE RESULTS

You have reached the finish line. You finished!!! How did you feel about completing the goal? Reaching the finish line? Did the feeling meet your expectations? How will you share it with others?

The result of my first master's degree was a degree and a graduation ceremony. My children both watched me walk across the stage. I did not attend my undergraduate graduation ceremony. For the next two, I was determined to graduate on stage because that was the result of the goal.

Now, you have crossed the finish line—the goal has been achieved. Now what? If there is more on the list, then repeat the process.

If this was a long-term goal, such as a business, then you have to ensure that it thrives. In this situation, there's not an actual finish line but several major checkpoints need to be addressed.

Now, the other part of the results is tracking what drives your success.

What motivates you?

What keeps you motivated?

What do you do to keep from getting off track?

Do you remain driven when times get tough?

Did you find the solution to any procrastination?

What is the significance of the results?

    Is there a trophy? A degree? A business card? A website?

The results are going to be profound. Amazing. Energetic. Electrifying. Fantastic.

In 90 Days

Did the results meet the expectations you desired or expected?

If so, then how?

If not, then why not?

REFLECTION

What motivates you?

_____
_____

What keeps you motivated?

_____
_____

What do you do to keep from getting off track?

_____
_____

Do you remain driven when times get tough?

_____
_____

Did you find the solution to any procrastination?

_____
_____

IN 90 DAYS

What is the significance of the results?

    Is there a trophy? A degree? A business card? A website?

_____

_____

Did the results meet the expectations you desired or expected? If so, then how? If not, then why not?

_____

_____

"In competition, your opponent has to view you as a threat. Otherwise, it's not a competition."

Onedia N. Gage

In 90 Days

THE CELEBRATION

At the twentieth published book, I scheduled a book celebration because someone asked me did I ever stop to celebrate my accomplishments. I blushed. I realized that I did not. I had stopped celebrating the moments, the results, and the accomplishments. In order to make my achievements mean something and to inspire others to do the same, I need to stop and celebrate my achievements.

What does your celebration look like for you for our goal?

For books, it is a book launch celebration. For a business, it is ribbon cutting. A baby requires a baby shower, a gender reveal, and in-hospital gift delivery. These are just examples of some celebrations. This is an area where you can borrow my ideas or create your own.

A celebration is necessary. It marks the milestone of accomplishment. It is an occasion to pause to recognize your effort, courage, and achievement.

You deserve that moment. Please do not rob yourself of it. It means something. What is the reward? Does it need to be extrinsic? In order to feel accomplished? There are some people who need incentives in order to produce normal results.

Reflection

How will you celebrate?

_____

_____

Who will you invite?

_____

_____

Who will help you organize the event?

_____

_____

"Life is too short to quit!

There is no reward for quitting.

There is only drive and determination for the tasks ahead.

Don't ever give up."

Onedia N. Gage

In 90 Days

90 Days Restarted

In exercise, the result of the goal of losing weight, you have to work out daily. Every day, you do something which puts you closer to the goal.

Sunday:	3 miles on the treadmill

Arm exercises

Abs

Monday:	3 miles on the bike

Leg exercises

Abs

Tuesday:	3 miles on the treadmill

Back exercises

Abs

Wednesday:	3 miles on the bike

Leg exercises

Abs

Thursday:	3 miles on the treadmill

Arm exercises

Abs

In 90 Days

Friday: 3 miles on the bike

Leg exercises

Abs

Saturday: 3 miles on the treadmill

Chest exercises

Abs

After about 12-13 weeks, the results of the daily workout with great effort and intensity in order to lose inches and pounds. 90 days are a critical threshold for success.

So, when you start for the next 90 days, you will need to start again but this start will be different because you know what you did not know before because of the last time.

You have learned some great things about yourself in the first 90 days that you did not know. You have grown and stretched into a place that you did not even know existed before now.

These next 90 days are the best decision you can immediately use what you have learned about yourself and your expanded capacity. This is essential to your capacity. This will influence what you do next.

REFLECTION

What have you learned about yourself during this season?

_____

_____

_____

_____

"The normal excuses are no longer effective.

Do your best!!!!

Stop letting yourself off of the hook."

Onedia N. Gage

90 Days in Review

In 90 days, what will you do? I am asked all of the time 'how do I do it.' Publishing. Authoring. Teaching. Parenting. Travel. Speaking. Educator.

Achieving miraculous accomplishments in record time is what I am asked all of the time. I make my efforts and achievements look easy. For that reason, I answer that question. I provide insight and guidance to others so that others can do the same.

I have written books, published books, earned degrees, bought a home, built a home, and some other exciting accomplishments all within 90 days.

If you take life in 90-day segments and provide the full spectrum of your effort and energy to something, then what can you really achieve?

You have nothing to lose by working hard toward your goals. You will only gain. You will understand your level of self-discipline and what that discipline yields. You must dedicate yourself to your life. You will only achieve your goals if you start to work on those goals right now.

As I consider how this changes your life and inspires you to be great, I am hoping that you continue to dream which becomes goals and achievements. I consider the opportunity to help others to do what I have done a great accomplishment for me as well. I believe that my empowering you is a great mentoring opportunity for both of us.

You are transforming from fear to fearless, from consumed with doubt to courageous, from a procrastinator to a performer. For that I am proud.

Most people don't realize that I do not lose anything by sharing what I know and what I have learned and have experienced. That is why I don't have a problem sharing what I know.

In 90 days, you have changed your life, your heart, your mind, your drive, your motivation, your mindset, your energy, and your elevated self-worth. You have shared your dreams, your skills, your ambitions, your fears, and your disbelief with people that you never anticipated and that sacrifice has yielded huge results—results that you never expected to experience.

The payback is to pay it forward.

REFLECTION

1. Who will you mentor?

___

___

2. Who will you share this book and its content with?

___

___

3. How will you continue to accomplish additional goals?

___

___

"When you look at the 5-year-old image of yourself, are you living the dreams of that 5-year-old?

If not, when will you start?

What will you do with that dream to start your reality?"

Onedia N. Gage

WHAT WILL YOU DO?

In 90 Days

APPENDIX

Dreams List   94

Goals List   95

Mission Statement   96

Vision Statement   100

Values Statement   104

Planning Calendars   106

In 90 Days

The Dreams List

THE GOALS LIST

The Mission Statement

A personal mission statement is based on habit 2 of <u>7 Habits of Highly Effective People</u> called begin with the end in mind. In one's life, the most effective way to begin with the end in mind is to develop a mission statement that focuses what you want to be in terms of character and what you want to do in reference to contribution of achievements. Writing a mission statement can be the most important activity an individual can take to truly lead one's life.

Victor Hugo once said there is nothing as powerful as an idea whose time has finally come, you may call it a credo, a philosophy, you may call it a purpose statement, it's not as important what you call it, it's how you define your definition. That mission and vision statement is more powerful, more significant, more influential, than the baggage of the past, or even the accumulated noise of the present.

What is a mission statement you ask? Personal mission statements based on correct principles are like a personal constitution, the basis for making major, life-directing decisions, the basis for making daily decisions in the midst of the circumstances and emotions that affect our lives.

Your statement may be a few words or several pages, but it is not a "to do" list. It reflects your uniqueness and must speak to you powerfully about the person you are and the person you are becoming.

Why should you write a personal mission statement?

Numerous experts on leadership and personal development emphasize how vital it is for you to craft your own personal vision for your life. Warren Bennis, Stephen Covey, Peter Senge, and others point out that a powerful vision can help you succeed far beyond where you'd be without one. That vision can propel you and inspire those around you to reach their own dreams.

Q: How do I go about creating my Personal Mission Statement?

A: A Mission Statement is defined as having goals and a deadline. This is opposed to the notion that a Mission Statement is just a bunch of flowery, general phrases like, "I will be the best business person I can be."

What should you include when writing a great personal mission statement?

- describe your best characteristics and how you express them
- have specific, measurable outcomes (or goals)
- have a deadline — for example, December 31st 2012, or a year from today.

When Stephen Covey talks about 'mission statement' in this quote, he is referring to the articulation of your life purpose. "If you don't set your goals based upon your Mission Statement, you may be climbing the ladder of success only to realize, when you get to the top, you're on the WRONG BUILDING." **Stephen Covey – 7 Habits of Highly Effective People.**

Mission Statement Example – Poor (It's more like a Vision Statement)

"I aspire to start my own business. I want to help others and be a better businesswoman. I will deliver the best food with the highest service levels." Jane

Mission Statement Example – Better

"I will start my business within 3 months and plan to grow it to $500,000 in revenues within a year. Using this success, my staff and I will spread the word to local schools and businesses about eco-friendly food production in order that we reach at least 100 people within the same time frame. My purpose will be to massively add value to our local community in measurable ways that have a real impact on people's health now and in the future," Jane.

What to do with your Mission Statement?

So now we have a mission, we can set a range of goals on the road to achieving your outcomes and dreams. Your values are clarified and should be in line with the goals you want to achieve in life so you should find it easier to make decisions and to do the "right thing" because you can simply ask yourself, "Will this help me achieve my mission?"

IN 90 DAYS

You can even put your mission statement in an area where your family or even co-workers will see it. For a mission statement defines who you are and what you stand for. This lets people see how you think and feel, which in turn, will help them respect, think and act in line with your values too.

WHAT WILL YOU DO?

THE MISSION STATEMENT

The Vision Statement

A personal vision/mission statement is the framework for creating a powerful life.

Your personal vision statement provides the direction necessary to guide the course of your days and the choices you make about your life.

The idea is to craft a broad based idea about your life and what will really make it exciting and fulfilling, that's your life vision.

From the vision, you craft a more focused and action orientated "mission" statement based on "purpose." And finally you get to a list of goals, wishes, desires and needs.

In his book 'The Success Principles,' Jack Canfield tells us that in order to create a balanced and successful life; your vision needs to include the following seven areas:

1. work and career
2. finances
3. recreation and free time
4. health and fitness
5. relationships
6. personal goals
7. contribution to the larger community

It does not include the distinctive ways that you intend to accomplish your purpose.

Why Write a Personal Vision Statement?

To express:

- your purpose
- your life's dream

- your core values & beliefs
- what you want for yourself
- what you want to contribute to others
- what you want to be

Characteristics of a Vision Statement:

- Engages your heart & spirit
- Taps into embedded concerns & needs
- Asserts what you want to create
- Is something worth going for
- Provides meaning to the work you do
- Is a little cloudy and grand
- Is simple
- Is a living document
- Provides a starting place from which to get more specificity
- Is based on quality and dedication

Key Elements of a Vision Statement:

- Written down and referred to daily
- Written in present tense, as if it has already been completed
- Includes a variety of activities and time frames
- Filled with descriptive details that anchor it to reality

What Visions Are Not:

- A mission statement: "Why do we exist now?"
- A strategic plan: "How do we plan to get there?"
- A set of objectives: "We will accomplish X by Y time to Z% target audience."

Use these questions to guide your thoughts:

- What are the ten things you most enjoy doing? Be honest. These are the ten things without which your weeks, months, and years would feel incomplete.

- What three things must you do every single day to feel fulfilled in your work?
- What are your five-six most important values?
- Your life has a number of important facets or dimensions, all of which deserve some attention in your personal vision statement.
- Write one important goal for each of them: physical, spiritual, work or career, family, social relationships, financial security, mental improvement and attention, and fun.
- If you never had to work another day in your life, how would you spend your time instead of working?
- When your life is ending, what will you regret not doing, seeing, or achieving?
- What strengths have other people commented on about you and your accomplishments? What strengths do you see in yourself?

WHAT WILL YOU DO?

THE VISION STATEMENT

The Values Statement

A personal **value** is absolute or relative and an ethical value, the assumption of which can be the basis for ethical action. A *value system* is a set of consistent values and measures. A *principle value* is a foundation upon which other values and measures of integrity are based.

Some values are physiologically determined and are normally considered objective, such as a desire to avoid physical pain or to seek pleasure. Other values are considered subjective, vary across individuals and cultures, and are in many ways aligned with belief and belief systems. Types of values include ethical/moral values, doctrinal/ideological (religious, political) values, social values, and aesthetic values. It is debated whether some values that are not clearly physiologically determined, such as altruism, are intrinsic, and whether some, such as acquisitiveness, should be classified as vices or virtues. Values have been studied in various disciplines: anthropology, behavioral economics, business ethics, corporate governance, moral philosophy, political sciences, social psychology, sociology, and theology to name a few.

Values can be defined as broad preferences concerning appropriate courses of action or outcomes. As such, values reflect a person's sense of right and wrong or what "ought" to be. "Equal rights for all", "Excellence deserves admiration", and "People should be treated with respect and dignity" are representative of values. Values tend to influence attitudes and behavior.

VALUES STATEMENT

Planning Calendars

Sun	Mon	Tue	Wed	Thu	Fri	Sat

WHAT WILL YOU DO?

	Sun	Mon	Tue	Wed	Thu	Fri	Sat

In 90 Days

Sun	Mon	Tue	Wed	Thu	Fri	Sat

WHAT WILL YOU DO?

Sun	Mon	Tue	Wed	Thu	Fri	Sat

In 90 Days

Sun	Mon	Tue	Wed	Thu	Fri	Sat

WHAT WILL YOU DO?

	Sun	Mon	Tue	Wed	Thu	Fri	Sat

IN 90 DAYS

	Sun	Mon	Tue	Wed	Thu	Fri	Sat

WHAT WILL YOU DO?

Sun	Mon	Tue	Wed	Thu	Fri	Sat

IN 90 DAYS

	Sun	Mon	Tue	Wed	Thu	Fri	Sat

WHAT WILL YOU DO?

	Sun	Mon	Tue	Wed	Thu	Fri	Sat

IN 90 DAYS

Sun	Mon	Tue	Wed	Thu	Fri	Sat

WHAT WILL YOU DO?

	Sun	Mon	Tue	Wed	Thu	Fri	Sat

In 90 Days

	Sun	Mon	Tue	Wed	Thu	Fri	Sat

WHAT WILL YOU DO?

In 90 Days

Acknowledgements

God, thank You for Your plans for me. Thank You for **In 90 Days: What Will You Do?** and for choosing me to complete Your project with the words that come out of my mouth. I just want to please You. Thank You for continuing to anoint me and to invest in me and my gifts, which keep surprising me. Thank You for loving and forgiving me.

Jordan and Nehemiah, thank you for supporting me and my endeavors. Thank you for loving me, especially when I do nothing without a pen and a clipboard, thank you for enduring my late nights, your ideas, the sounding board, the love, and the support. Thank you for celebrating our legacy.

To my prayer partners and to my accountability partners, thank you for the long talks, the powerful prayers, and the encouragement. To my pastor and church family, thank you so much for your love and support.

In 90 Days

Onedia N. Gage seeks to share her outlandish pursuit of life with her work ethic. She de___ to share her achievements in a manner which helps you do the same through her exam___ hopes that these words will motivate you ___

Please feel free to contact and share your progress. onediagage@onediagespeaks.com, o___ @onediangage (twitter). www.___speaks.com

Blogtalkradio.com/onediagage

Youtube.com/onediagage

Facebook.com/onediagage

In 90 Days

WHAT WILL YOU DO?

COACH ♦ ADVOCATE ♦ TEACHER ♦ FACILITATOR

CONFERENCE SPEAKER ♦ WORKSHOP LEADER

To invite Dr. Gage to speak at your school, business, or organization,

Please contact us at: www.onedigagespeaks.com

@onediangage (twitter) ♦ onediagage@onediagagespeaks.com ♦ facebook.com/onediagage

youtube.com/onediagage ♦ blogtalkradio.com/onediagage ♦ ongage (Instagram)

In 90 Days

Publishing

Do you have a book you want to write, but do not know what to do?

Do you have a book you need to publish but do not know how to start?

Would publishing move your career forward?

Let us help

onediagage@purpleink.net ♦ www.purpleink.net

281.740.5143 ♦ 713.705.5530

www.ingramcontent.com/pod-product-compliance
Lightning Source LLC
Chambersburg PA
CBHW081750100526
44592CB00015B/2371